LOOS SAVE LIVES

How sanitation and clean water help prevent poverty, disease and death

Seren Boyd

toilet twinning.org

WAYLAND

About Toilet Twinning

A third of the people in the world today don't have access to a proper toilet.

That's about 2.4 billion people ... and that stinks!

Most of these people are living in poverty in low-income countries. Toilet Twinning wants them to have life-saving loos, clean water and all the information they need to stay clean and healthy. So, we invite people who are fortunate enough to have these things to 'twin' their toilet so other people can have them too – at home, in school and in displacement camps.

Having a toilet changes people's lives. Their health improves so they have more time and energy for work, such as farming. This means they can earn more and spend less on medicines, so they can afford to send their children to school. Toilets in schools keep children – and especially girls – in education.

Loos give people privacy, keep them safe and protect their dignity. We train and equip people to build their own toilets, and they're always very proud of them. So, toilets can make people feel more confident and more hopeful too. Whole communities are being transformed, one toilet at a time.

Why not talk to your teacher or family about doing some fundraising so you can twin your toilet at school or at home? In return for your £60 donation you'll receive a certificate with a photo of your toilet twin and its precise location, so you can hang it in your privy with pride. Ask an adult to help you donate online at:
www.toilettwinning.org

Toilet Twinning is part of the international development agency, Tearfund.

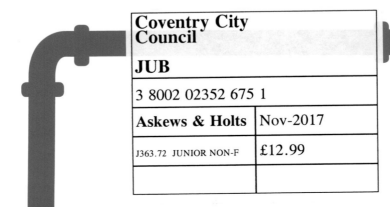

Contents

Words in **bold** can be found in the glossary on pages 30–31.

LIFE-SAVING LOOS

Have you ever thought that you are lucky to have a toilet at home? Do you wonder what life would be like without one? We often take it for granted that we have toilets at home and at school. We do our business and flush, without a second thought. In fact, loos are a very important part of our lives. They keep us clean, healthy and safe – which helps us stay alive!

NO LAUGHING MATTER

We may find it embarrassing or funny to talk about 'number twos' (poos). Yet for 2.4 billion people in the world today, it's no laughing matter. Not having access to a proper loo means they may have to relieve themselves outside in the open, even when it's dark or not safe.

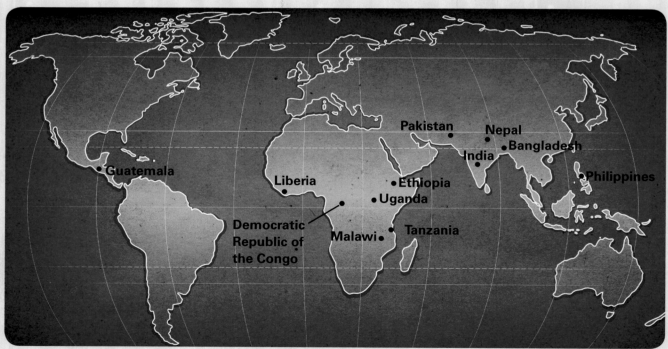

This map shows the countries mentioned in this book.

SANITATION

Diseases spread quickly in places where there's no proper sanitation (the removal and safe disposal of **human waste**) or where people don't have access to clean water. People fall ill and can't work, which means they have less money for the food and medicine they need to survive. Children miss lessons or drop out of school altogether. Sadly, every year, many people die simply because they don't have somewhere safe and clean to go to the toilet.

Stinking stat

Almost 900 children die every day from diseases caused by not having access to a proper loo or clean water. That's one child every two minutes.

TRANSFORMATION

But when families get their first loo, their lives change dramatically. Sometimes the whole community is transformed! Whatever you call yours – the loo or the lav, the bathroom or the bog – it's time we started to think differently about the humble toilet.

A Guatemalan family stand proudly outside their new loo.

Imagine ...
... if you had to go to the toilet outside, in the street or in your garden. How would you feel?

WHERE'S THE LOO?

Why don't billions of people have a proper toilet? They may not have the materials and skills they need to build one or they may not know that they need one to stay healthy. Whatever the reason, they have one thing in common – they live in **poverty**.

MONEY MATTERS

Billions of people are so poor that a toilet can seem like an unaffordable **luxury** to them. Any money they do have tends to be spent on food and shelter. Even if they had spare cash, they might not realise that a well-built toilet could make a huge difference to their health.

Without a loo, many are likely to become trapped in a cycle of becoming gradually poorer, weaker and sicker. This costs them time and money and can also mean:

- they miss work or school
- they earn less or grow less food
- they have to pay for medicine
- they might fall into **debt** and end up having to pay back more money than they borrowed.

OTHER FACTORS

Conflict or war often drives people from their homes. Others may lose everything because of **natural disasters** (see pages 18-19). These people are often forced to live on the streets, in **displacement camps** where sanitation can be limited (or non-existent) or in makeshift shelters without proper toilets.

A young girl sits outside her makeshift tent in a displacement camp in Pakistan.

Ebinda (far left) and her family are much safer now, thanks to their new loo.

CASE STUDY: CONFLICT IN CENTRAL AFRICA

Ebinda's father was killed during a **civil war** in the Democratic Republic of Congo. The rest of the family fled to Tanzania in East Africa and spent ten years there in a refugee camp. When they were returned to their own country, they had no home, no clean water and no toilet.

As a teenager, Ebinda had to walk for 90 minutes, three times a day, to collect water from Lake Tanganyika. But the water was dirty and many people got the disease **cholera** after drinking it. The fighting hadn't stopped either. One day, Ebinda was attacked by several men when she went to the toilet in the **bush** (see pages 24-25). She spent three days in hospital.

Her country is still troubled by conflict, but Ebinda is much safer now. Toilet Twinning helped provide a **borehole**, which brings clean water to the village. Her family have built a home and, best of all, their neighbours built them a toilet. Her mother, Bawili, says, 'We used to be ashamed when people shouted **abuse** as we walked to the bush. I'm so happy to have a toilet.'

Stinking stat
One billion people have to go to the toilet outside, in the open or behind a bush.

Flushable fact
The total global cost of people not having a proper toilet is about £207 billion a year. That's almost double the amount the world gives in **aid money** to help **low-income** countries develop.

DIRT AND DISEASE

In many countries, people are forced to go to the loo outside (open defecation) or have to use a bag or a bucket to go to the toilet. If human waste is not dealt with safely, it can become a serious health hazard.

SPREADING ILLNESS

Worms in the intestines (gut) make millions of people sick and stop children from growing properly. Infected people have worm eggs in their **faeces**. Where sanitation is poor, these eggs can pass from person to person, often in **contaminated** soil.

Roundworms can live in the gut for up to two years.

Even a single gram of faeces contains millions of **viruses** and **bacteria**, which can be harmful. When human waste is left lying about, people with bare feet may tread on it or young children may touch it. If it gets into a cut or the mouth, it can cause infection. Faeces also attract flies, which land on it, then crawl over people's skin or food.

All this spreads disease, especially **diarrhoea**. People with diarrhoea can quickly **dehydrate** and need to drink lots of clean water, mixed with sugar and salt. Without this, they can die – especially infants and elderly people whose **immune systems** are weak.

These children in the Philippines are eating fly-infested food from a rubbish dump.

GOOD GUYS, BAD GUYS

Germs are a type of **microbe**. Microbes are tiny **organisms** that are everywhere: in the soil, in the air, on our skin and in our gut. In the right place, most microbes are harmless and do important jobs, such as digesting our food. Germs though, such as flu viruses and some bad bacteria, are harmful microbes and can cause disease.

Flushable fact

The average man has about 40,000,000,000,000 (40 trillion) bacteria in his body.

Mira with her father, Bishwo

CASE STUDY: A NASTY TURN IN NEPAL

Mira is 20 and lives in the foothills of the Himalayas in Nepal. When she was a teenager she fell seriously ill. She was in hospital for a month and missed a lot of school.

Mira's family didn't realise that their own toilet waste was making them ill. Their toilet was built too close to the stream where they got their drinking water, and was contaminating the water with bacteria.

When Toilet Twinning partners taught Mira's father, Bishwo, how to build a proper loo in the right place, he sold two of his goats to pay for the materials. He was so proud of his new loo that he held an open day and invited neighbours to try out his toilet. Many of his neighbours have since built a toilet for themselves. 'My toilet is my guarantee of old age!' says Bishwo.

Imagine ...
... if your drinking water was contaminated by your toilet water!

HANDWASHING AND HYGIENE

Practising good **hygiene** is the best way to stop germs spreading. Our hands are ideal habitats for bacteria – including some harmful ones – so washing your hands is one of the most effective weapons against disease.

UNSEEN ENEMIES

FIVE TIMES

There are five occasions when you should always wash your hands:

- before preparing food
- before eating
- after using the loo
- after wiping or cleaning a baby
- after playing or working outside.

Things around us may look clean, but many are actually covered in germs and sometimes even tiny bits of poo. When we touch things, such as a door handle or smartphone, our hands pick up and transfer germs, which can make us sick. Washing our hands with soap and water helps lift dirt and germs off our skin. So, if we're to stay healthy, sanitation should always go hand-in-hand with good hygiene.

Flushable fact

The average smartphone has more germs on it than the average loo seat.

CASE STUDY: BARE ESSENTIALS

Sembeto is five and lives in a simple mud hut with his mum, Kibnesh, and granny Tirame (left) in a village in Ethiopia. They don't have flushing toilets or **sewage** pipes. Their toilet is a **latrine**. Their clean water for washing, cooking and drinking comes from a **tapstand** they share with neighbours. Sembeto's mum washes him in a tub.

FIVE STEPS TO CLEAN HANDS

1. Wet hands.

2. Add soap and rub to create a lather.

3. Wash hands, wrists and under fingernails for at least 15 seconds.

4. Rinse hands under running water.

5. Dry hands with a paper towel and use the towel to turn off the tap.

TIPPY TAPS

Sembeto washes his hands using clean water stored in a plastic bottle hanging from a stick. His neighbour, Adanech, has an even better solution called a tippy tap. She steps on a pedal attached to her bottle with string, and this makes the bottle tilt to release a small amount of water. She doesn't have to touch the tap with her hands at all. If soap isn't available, ash or sand are used instead as the gritty texture helps to remove dirt.

TOILET CHAMPIONS IN LIBERIA

The deadly **Ebola** virus began to sweep through West Africa in 2014. It spread fast as people came into contact with body fluids, such as sweat and **urine**, from infected people. But in Liberia, the worst affected country, most people didn't know how it spread. Later they learnt that handwashing could help stop the virus in its tracks – but for many people it was too late.

FRIGHTENING TIMES

Special clinics were set up across West Africa to deal with the Ebola crisis (left).

A magnified view of the Ebola virus

The virus spread terrifyingly quickly. Many fell ill after caring for sick relatives because they had no idea how Ebola spread. Even some doctors and nurses refused to work, out of fear for their lives. Many health clinics closed, just when they were needed the most.

FRESH START

The Ebola crisis was terrible and sad. But people in Liberia started to learn how important handwashing and hygiene are in helping to prevent the spread of the disease. Now children help play an important role in spreading life-saving information.

CLEAN COMMUNITIES

Dorothy, 14, will never forget the time of the Ebola crisis. At her school in Bong, central Liberia, Dorothy is part of a new health club. Its members teach other pupils to wash their hands properly at the new handwashing stands and keep their fingernails short to prevent dirt and germs getting trapped underneath them.

Children are proud to take turns to clean the school loos and playground. They've even started teaching good hygiene to children at other schools – and to their families.

Many families are building toilets for the first time, including Dorothy's. Dorothy knows she's making a difference in her community and that makes her feel happy and confident. Before, she thought poorer children like her weren't as clever as children from the city. 'We thought they knew it all,' she says. 'Now we too are experienced in talking about a safe, clean environment.'

Dorothy (above, left) and her school health club show off their clean hands.

Flushable fact

There's only one doctor for about every 19,000 patients in Liberia. In the UK, there is one for about every 360 people and in the US about one for every 344 people.

Stinking stat

Almost 5,000 people in Liberia died of Ebola in 2014–2015. Across West Africa, more than 11,300 people died.

WATER AND CONTAMINATION

The water cycle is nature's way of recycling water so that our supply of fresh water is continually replenished. However, the amount of fresh water available to us is shrinking because of contamination. In some parts of the world, fresh water is becoming harder to find.

PRECIOUS RESOURCE

Only one per cent of all the world's water is the fresh water that we consume. Some of it covers Earth's surface as lakes and rivers, the rest is underground. Most of the remaining water is salty ocean water that we can't drink. The water on Earth is constantly changing form as it journeys through the water cycle, but the total amount stays the same.

THE WATER CYCLE

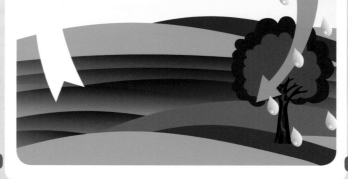

2. As the **water vapour** rises, it forms clouds.

3. Precipitation, such as rain or snow, falls onto the land and into rivers, lakes and the sea.

1. When the Sun shines, water on the land and in the sea **evaporates**.

HARMING OUR WATER

The amount of fresh water available is shrinking because of contamination. This happens in several ways:

- rubbish dumps create **toxic waste** that seeps into the soil and rivers
- factories and industries tip chemicals into drains and waterways
- **pesticides** and **fertilisers** used in farming pollute rivers
- untreated sewage is pumped into rivers and the ocean.

Toxic waste flowing into our fresh water supplies is contaminating them.

LONG WALK

In low-income countries, people don't have **purified** water piped into their homes. They may have to walk a long way – six km on average – to find water, especially if there's a **drought** (see pages 18–19). Often, the water they collect is contaminated, or it's buzzing with disease-carrying mosquitos that lay their eggs there.

Imagine ...

... how you might change the way you used water if you had to walk many kilometres to collect it.

EVERYONE'S PROBLEM

Water contamination is not just a problem in low-income countries. In **developed countries**, factories, farmers and even gardeners can contribute to contamination. We're *all* responsible for keeping our fresh water clean.

Stinking stat

Every day, two million tonnes of sewage and other waste water drain into the world's rivers and seas.

OPERATION CLEAN-UP IN GUATEMALA

The tropical climate in Guatemala, Central America, makes villages like San Juan Mocá hot and humid. During the wet season, rainwater gushes down the hillsides, and children splash in the mud. There is no shortage of water here but contamination has been a real problem, until now.

CONTAMINATED WATER

Jeremías is 11. He has lived in San Juan Mocá all his life. The River Mocá has always been at the centre of village life. Although villagers sometimes drank the river's water, they also washed and bathed and sometimes went to the toilet in it. The few latrines in the village were badly designed, with sewage pipes leading directly into the river. People often fell ill.

The villagers didn't realise that they were contaminating the river water. They also didn't know that leaving water in open containers attracts mosquitos that help to spread diseases. San Juan Mocá has no doctor and few families can afford medicines. Some people have died after drinking dirty water, including Jeremías' older sister.

One of Jeremías' neighbours washes her clothes in the River Mocá.

ECO-FILTERS

Now that Toilet Twinning is working in San Juan Mocá, the villagers know that clean water helps keep them healthy. Most of them now clean their drinking water with an eco-filter. The filter is a pot made of clay and sawdust. The clay contains chemicals to remove bacteria. Water poured into the pot takes one or two hours to become clean. The pot sits inside a large plastic container with a tap, where the clean drinking water comes out. Before local families had filters, they had to boil water to make it safe to drink, which meant gathering firewood. **Deforestation** is a serious problem in Guatemala.

Jeremías and his mother, Reina, are much happier and healthier now they have a new loo.

TEAM EFFORT

Living in San Juan Mocá is much healthier for everyone now that the villagers are taking better care of their water. They have started building proper toilets – with pits for the sewage. 'I helped my grandad build our toilet,' Jeremías says proudly. 'I dug the pit with him.' The hope is that one day soon no one in the village will drink water straight from the river or use it as a toilet.

Luis, another of Jeremías' neighbours, uses an eco-filter to get himself a glass of clean water.

Stinking stat
In Guatemala, one million people in rural areas do not have clean drinking water.

EXTREME WEATHER AND NATURAL DISASTERS

Humans are not always to blame for water contamination. Nature often causes problems too. When extreme weather or natural disasters strike, accessing fresh water can become even harder. Whether there's too little water or far too much, diseases can spread quickly, making a bad situation far worse.

CRUEL CLIMATE

Hot weather can make it harder to keep clean. Rising temperatures can make germs multiply and disease-carrying insects breed faster. Heavy rains can cause flooding, which contaminates clean water with human waste and chemicals.

Sometimes weather is so extreme that it can cause a natural disaster. For example, a long period of dry weather can lead to drought, food shortages and even **famine**. Most scientists believe that **climate change** is making extreme weather more common and more intense.

CHALLENGES FOR SURVIVORS

Other natural disasters also put clean water supplies at risk. **Earthquakes** can damage pipes carrying water or sewage. During **tsunamis**, seawater floods the land, contaminating fresh water.

People often lose their homes in a natural disaster and take shelter in displacement camps. Where so many people are living close together, often without proper sanitation, water supplies easily become contaminated. This, combined with a lack of washing facilities, means water-borne diseases, such as cholera, spread fast.

Flushable fact

Often it is the rapid spread of disease that kills more people after a natural disaster than the disaster itself.

Kalpana and her family survived the 2015 earthquake in Nepal.

CASE STUDY: DISASTER STRIKES NEPAL

Kalpana is a teacher. She lives in Bahungaun village, high in the mountains of Nepal. To get there means turning off the main road from Hetadu to Kathmandu, driving for two-and-a-half-hours on a very rough track, then walking for half an hour. When a very strong earthquake struck Nepal in April 2015, more than half the houses in the Bahungaun area were damaged or destroyed. In total, eight million people in Nepal were affected and **tremors** were felt in nearby countries, including India and China.

The earthquake blocked **natural springs** and damaged water pipes in Bahungaun. Only one tap in Kalpana's village worked after the quake, and the water was muddy. The queues at the tap were so long that some people drank contaminated water from a stream.

Rescue teams trekked for hours to reach remote villages like Bahungaun. First, they handed out tablets and filters so people could clean their drinking water. Then they found a new spring, an hour's walk away, and connected it to a water tank in Bahungaun. They also taught villagers how to test the water and check it was clean. Kalpana's water supply is safer now than it was before the quake. 'Now we can get water easily, I have time to help my children with their homework,' she says.

The 2015 earthquake in Nepal left entire villages in ruins.

Imagine ...
... what it might be like to experience a severe earthquake.

LOOS AND LEARNING

Schools are busy places, packed with people, where germs spread easily. Less than half of schools in low-income countries have proper, clean toilets. So, pupils regularly fall ill and miss lessons, and evidence shows that their school results are affected.

STUMBLING BLOCKS

In schools without proper toilets, children are at high risk of infection, especially from intestinal worms (see page 8). Regular worm infections can cause children not to eat or grow properly and it has been medically proven that this may lead to children having a lower **IQ**. Worm infections can cause children to miss almost a quarter of their lessons.

Hookworms are estimated to infect over 700 million people around the world. .

Millions of children around the world do not finish primary school.

A child who is often absent is more likely to drop out of school altogether. Children from the poorest families in low-income countries – and especially girls (see pages 22-23) – are already under pressure to stay at home to help their parents. Families have to pay for uniforms and school books and putting food on the table comes first.

RIPPLE EFFECT

Keeping children in education is important for everyone. A child who stays in school has a better chance of getting a good job and earning a decent wage. If more children stay in school longer, it creates a ripple effect where living standards improve, the country's economy grows and the whole country benefits.

Flushable fact

57 million children of school age are not in school in low-income countries. More than half of them live in sub-Saharan Africa.

Stinking stat

Children worldwide miss a total of 443 million school days a year because of dirty water or poor sanitation.

CASE STUDY: SCHOOLS TRANSFORMED IN UGANDA

Most people in Bridget's village in southwest Uganda are banana farmers. Fourteen-year-old Bridget (above, left) wants to be a nurse. She knows she must do well at school. But only one in three Ugandan children completes primary education. Bridget lives in Rukungiri, one of the country's poorest areas.

Children like Bridget have to help out at home and at school. Bridget and her classmates used to take turns to collect water from a contaminated spring over a kilometre away. They missed lessons and fell behind. The old school toilets were 'disgusting', says Bridget.

But now the school has a tapstand so the children no longer miss class to get water. The girls also have their own toilets, thanks to Toilet Twinning. Now the school is clean, children's attendance is much better and so are Bridget's chances of becoming a nurse. 'To achieve my goal, I need to stay healthy,' she says.

A FAIR DEAL FOR GIRLS

Safe, private toilets in school are particularly important for girls, especially when they reach **puberty**. A lack of facilities means many teenage girls drop out of education altogether. That's if they go to school at all ...

BAD MARKS

Staying in school can be a challenge for many girls.

During their monthly **period**, girls need clean water and somewhere safe and private to wash. Many families cannot afford sanitary towels so some girls use bits of cloth instead, which they may need to wash and reuse many times. If there are no toilets at school, each girl can miss school for up to a week a month – a quarter of their education. They cannot catch up, so they may fail tests and exams and many drop out of school completely.

In sub-Saharan Africa, less than half of girls are still in class by the end of primary school. Girls who drop out are much more likely to get married early and become young mums. Because their bodies are not fully developed, pregnancy and childbirth can be risky for them and their babies are less likely to survive.

Stinking stat
Two-thirds of all the people in the world who cannot read or write are female.

Flushable fact

About 16 million teenage girls give birth each year.

BOYS FIRST

If parents can't afford to send all their children to school, they're more likely to send sons than daughters. Men traditionally have more job opportunities open to them, in roles that some women are not allowed to do or are discouraged from doing. Because boys tend to stay in school for longer, they gain better qualifications and so get better jobs where they are paid better salaries.

Imagine ...
... if most girls in your class dropped out of school to help their parents at home.

CASE STUDY: BACK TO SCHOOL IN BANGLADESH

Suma was a good student and never missed school ... until puberty. Her school in the far north of Bangladesh had only one toilet for 341 girls. The boys had no toilet at all.

Suma poses in her school uniform next to the new girls' toilet block at her school.

Suma's mum didn't let her go to school during her period. Some of the girls used to go to nearby houses to change, but this meant they missed lessons, and some were afraid they might be attacked by men as they changed.

'Missing school was really painful for me,' says Suma, who's 14. She started falling behind. Suma's parents are so poor that they work on other farms as well as their own to earn enough to survive. But they really wanted Suma to continue her studies.

Everything changed for Suma when the new toilet blocks were built at Baromari School – one for boys, one for girls – through Toilet Twinning. Attendance has risen and drop-out rates have fallen. Many more girls have enrolled. 'Now I never miss classes,' says Suma. 'I'm very proud of my school.'

PRIVIES = PRIVACY AND PROTECTION

Protecting women's modesty is so important in some countries that women and girls have to wait until it is dark before they can go to the loo outside. Going to the toilet can be frightening and dangerous. Having a toilet at home keeps women safe and protects their dignity.

LURKING IN THE DARK

In countries such as India, women and girls cannot be seen going to the loo outside. Women's modesty is very important for Hindu people, especially in more traditional, rural areas. So women and girls have to venture out before dawn or late at night. It can be scary.

When people are squatting in the dark, it's hard to see creatures, such as snakes including the Russell's viper (top left) and scorpions lurking in the undergrowth – and harder still to get away fast. Larger animals, such as lions, tigers and wolves, also hunt at night. Sometimes, other people lie in wait to attack women (see Ebinda's story, page 7).

During daylight hours, when they can't go outside to the toilet, women simply have to hold on. This can cause stress, pain and health problems, such as liver infections and **constipation**. Women often eat and drink less to stop themselves needing to go to the loo.

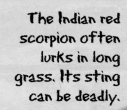
The Indian red scorpion often lurks in long grass. Its sting can be deadly.

Stinking stat

People in low-income countries spend on average the equivalent of two -and-a -half days a year trying to find somewhere safe to go to the toilet.

CASE STUDY: NIGHT-TIME TREKS IN INDIA

Niva, 14, lives in northeast India. All around her village are rice fields. Floods are common in Bihar state and toilets are rare, so disease spreads fast. Many people don't understand that this is why their children fall sick. They blame 'evil spirits' instead.

In the early morning, the men squat by the roadside to go to the toilet, as people in India have done for centuries. But the women have to go during the hours of darkness. Niva is fortunate as she has a toilet at home now. But she remembers when she used to have to go out into the fields before dawn. 'All the ladies used to go out together at about 5.30 a.m.,' Niva says. 'But I worried about snakes. I don't like the dark.'

Across India, more and more women and girls have had enough of these night-time treks. Many have joined the 'No toilet, no bride' campaign and refuse to marry until their husband-to-be builds them a loo.

India's 'No toilet, no bride' campaign has hit the headlines.

शौचालय नहीं रहने पर ससुराल

समाज को संदेश

र्तिहार | हिन्दुस्तान संवाददाता

री सशक्तीकरण के दौर में कटिहार
क एक युवती ने भले अपने ससुराल
से नाता तोड़ लिया, लेकिन उसने एक
बड़ा संदेश इस समाज को भी दिया
कुरसेला नवाबगंज की बेटी

उस स्लोगन को चरितार्थ किया
जिसमें कहा गया है कि 'बेटी दो उस
घर में शौचालय हो जिस घर में'।
इसके साथ ही उसने नारी मन की उस
पीड़ा को भी उजागर किया की घर में
घूंघट सड़क पर शौच।
नवाबगंज पूरब टोला के स्व. राम
मंडल की बेटी यशोदा की शादी
सेमापुर सकरैली के सहदेव मंडल के
पुत्र प्रकाश मंडल के साथ 11 महीने

यशोदा देवी।

यशोदा अपने ससुराल वालों से
शौचालय बनाने को लेकर लगा

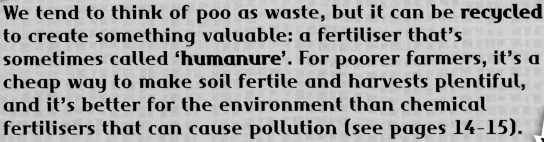

HUMANURE AND POO POWER

We tend to think of poo as waste, but it can be **recycled** to create something valuable: a fertiliser that's sometimes called '**humanure**'. For poorer farmers, it's a cheap way to make soil fertile and harvests plentiful, and it's better for the environment than chemical fertilisers that can cause pollution (see pages 14-15).

COMPOSTING TOILETS

Urine and faeces contain **nutrients**, such as nitrogen, which plants need to grow. Before it is safe to use as fertiliser, human waste needs to be turned into **compost**. In composting toilets, for example, ash is added to the pit to create a safe, dry compost. In other toilet designs, the human waste is transferred to a separate, shallow pit so warmth from the Sun can dry it out.

Communities that use humanure successfully are seeing better harvests, which means families have more food to eat and can earn more money selling any extra crops they grow. Not everyone likes the idea of growing crops using humanure but, in many countries, treated sewage has been used as a fertiliser for centuries. Humanure is purer than treated sewage because it isn't contaminated by the chemicals dumped into drains (see page 15).

This composting loo in India is built over a raised pit.

Potato

Even young childern like Bruce help in the fields in Uganda. Here he is helping to harvest his poo-powered potatoes!

The soil is becoming less fertile however, and drought, floods and crop diseases have led to poor harvests. Bruce's mother, Apophia, has recently started using humanure from the composting toilet at her local church. The crops they've grown – including potatoes, beans and bananas – have been bigger and better than usual.

CASE STUDY: BUMPER HARVESTS IN UGANDA

There are eight children in Bruce's family in south-west Uganda. That's a lot of mouths to feed! The family grow their own food and raise money for school fees by selling crops. Everyone lends a hand, even Bruce, who's seven. 'I like to be useful – and I love corn-on-the-cob!' he says.

Bruce's family is encouraging friends and neighbours to use humanure too. Onyete's family are already on board. Onyete is at university, but when he's home he still helps on the farm. He was worried at first about using humanure – but not now. 'I thought the crops it produced would smell and not be fit to eat, but the bananas we grew with humanure were even sweeter than normal!' he says.

Stinking stats
Every year, people in developed countries waste almost as much food (222 million tonnes) as the whole of sub-Saharan Africa produces in a year (230 million tonnes).

Flushable fact
Britain recycles more than three-quarters of its sewage onto farm land. More than half of the USA's sewage is used in agriculture – about four million tonnes of it each year.

TOILET TRIVIA

Here are a few toilet-related truths to amaze your friends ... but perhaps not at mealtimes.

- One gram of poo can contain ten million viruses and one million bacteria.

- Three-quarters of our poo is made up of water. The rest is a mixture of fibre, dead cells, fats and bacteria.

- The average human produces almost one kg of poo a day. The average elephant produces a mighty 36 kg!

- 'Poo buses', powered entirely by gas extracted from human and food waste, now run in the UK, France and Sweden.

- During the Second World War (1939-1945), German tank drivers thought it brought them good luck to drive over camel dung. They were wrong. The British army disguised landmines as camel dung and lots of German tanks were blown up before they worked out the British tactic.

- Old toilets can use up to 26 litres of water per flush. Even the most efficient toilets use four litres per flush.

ANIMAL ANTICS

- Up to 70 per cent of white sand on beaches in the Caribbean is made of parrotfish poo.

- Sloths go to the toilet just once a week.

- In the past, dog poo and human wee were used to treat animal skins and produce leather.

- The Japanese use rare nightingale poo as a beauty treatment. Ancient Romans used to dye their hair with pigeon poo.

toilet twinning.org

WORLD TOILET DAY is on **19 NOVEMBER** every year – a great day to celebrate your loo and twin it with a toilet overseas

UN WATER
19 November
WORLD TOILET DAY

A POTTED HISTORY OF THE TOILET

* Some people believe that Skara Brae, the Stone Age settlement on Orkney had the first indoor toilet.

* During the Bronze Age, the Minoans (about 3650 to 1400 BCE) built an early 'flush' toilet on the island of Crete.

* The 'pig toilet' in China dates back to the Han dynasty (206 BCE to CE 220). It's a simple loo mounted above a pigsty: human waste drops down through a hole so the pigs can eat it.

* The ancient Romans built toilets in rows so people looked like they were sitting on a bench together. Businessmen often met in the toilet to do business while they ... did their business. (You can still see the loos at the Roman fort of Vindolanda in Northumberland, and they're twinned too!)

* In medieval Europe, people used to throw the contents of their chamber pots (adult potties) out of the window into the street below. The French would shout *'Guarde à l'eau!'* ('Watch out for the water!'). The British turned this phrase into 'gardy-loo', then shortened it to 'loo'.

* Even in Queen Victoria's time (1819-1901), people didn't know the link between sanitation and disease until Dr John Snow discovered that cholera was being spread through a London water pump in 1854. After Victoria's husband, Albert, died in 1861, apparently of the water-borne disease **typhoid**, Queen Victoria called for water and sewage treatment across the UK.

STRANGE BUT TRUE ...

* Toilets on a space station, where weightlessness causes everything to float, use a suction pump to ensure astronauts' wee doesn't float around the space station!

* The Guggenheim Museum in New York contains a useable toilet made of 24-carat gold.

* Many health experts say the best way to use a toilet is to squat, not sit – because our bowel muscles relax and we get rid of our waste more efficiently. While we in the West sit, most of the rest of the world squats.

GLOSSARY

abuse — to say or do hurtful things to someone

aid money — money sent from one country's government to another to help a country develop or pay for emergency resources

bacteria — single-celled microbes that can only be seen under a microscope. Most bacteria are not harmful but some can cause disease.

borehole — a hole drilled to reach water deep underground

bush — wild, rural land that is not farmed, for example in Africa or Australia

cholera — a highly infectious and often fatal disease caused by bacteria and typically spread through infected water; causes severe vomiting and diarrhoea

civil war — a war between citizens of the same country

climate change — a change in Earth's weather patterns that is causing our planet to warm up more quickly than it should

compost — organic matter that has decomposed and turned into a nutrient-rich type of soil

conflict — fighting or tension between groups of people

constipation — difficulty passing faeces from the bowel, often because they are hard and dry

contaminate — to cause water or the environment to become dirty or 'infected', for example when human waste mixes with clean water in a river

debt — a sum of money that is owed to another person or organisation

deforestation — clearing or cutting down forests for humans' use

dehydrate — to lose a large amount of water from the body

developed country — a country where there is well-developed industry and infrastructure and most of the population have a reasonably high standard of living

diarrhoea — passing watery faeces regularly, often because of diseases linked to poor sanitation and dirty water

displacement camp — these camps temporarily house people who have been forced from their homes, usually due to conflict, extreme weather or natural disasters

drought — a shortage of rain over a long period of time

earthquake — a sudden and often violent shaking of the ground when the tectonic plates that make up Earth's crust move about

Ebola — a highly infectious and often fatal disease caused by the Ebola virus

evaporate — when water turns from liquid into vapour as it heats up

faeces — solid waste from the body; also called poo

famine — a very great shortage of food that affects many people over a wide area, usually causing sickness and death

fertiliser — nutrients added to soil to help plants grow

germs — harmful microbes that cause sickness and disease

human waste — solid and liquid waste (faeces and urine) from the human body

humanure — human waste that's been treated and broken down into a fertiliser that can be added safely to farmland

hygiene — habits that prevent disease and protect health, especially through keeping clean and washing

IQ — Intelligence Quotient; a way of assessing someone's intelligence

immune system — the way the human body fights infection and disease

latrine — a simple design of toilet, used in many low-income countries, where a slab with a hole in it covers a deep pit

low-income country — a country where there is little industry or infrastructure and most of the population have a reasonably low standard of living

luxury — something that is not an essential item and is usually expensive to buy

microbe — a micro-organism (tiny living thing) found in the air, water and our bodies

natural disaster — a disaster that results from a natural event, such as a tsunami or an earthquake

natural spring — a place where water held in rocks underground bubbles up to the surface

nutrient — a substance that is vital to help bodies or plants grow and stay healthy

organism — an individual animal, plant or other life form

period — the flow of blood and other material from the uterus out of the vagina, experienced by girls and women approximately once every month from puberty; also called menstruation

pesticides — chemicals which farmers put on their crops to kill harmful insects and weeds

poverty — the state of being extremely poor

precipitation	rain, snow, sleet or hail that falls to the ground	**toxic waste**	waste, especially from factories, that is harmful to people's health or the environment
puberty	the time of life when a child's body reaches sexual maturity and is able to reproduce	**tremor**	a small earthquake
purify	to remove dirt, toxins or other substances from something	**tsunami**	a long, high and dangerous sea wave often caused by an earthquake
recycle	to change a waste product into something useable	**typhoid**	an infectious fever caused by bacteria, typically spread through food or water contaminated with faeces
sewage	waste water from humans and their houses, including toilet waste	**urine**	liquid waste from the body; also called wee
sub-Saharan Africa	African countries that lie south of the Sahara Desert	**virus**	a type of microbe that causes disease and is often spread easily between people
tapstand	an outside tap which may be used by a single family or many people	**water vapour**	water in its invisible gassy form; part of the water cycle

Toilet Twinning wants everyone to have a toilet – and to keep on using it. So, first, it teaches the community why toilets are so important. Next, it discusses with local families where and how to build them. Toilet Twinning gives people training and materials, but the families dig the pits, install the slabs and build walls for privacy. They're the ones who do the hard work and make change happen!

Remember! Toilet Twinning loos won't look exactly like the toilet you use at home or at school. Generally, they are simple latrines, where the waste drops down into a pit, and people squat to use them, rather than sitting down. But even the most basic latrine can change lives for the better – because loos really do save lives!

INDEX

First published in Great Britain in 2017 by Wayland
Text © Seren Boyd 2017
All rights reserved.
Editor: Amy Pimperton
Designer: Akihiro Nakayama
Picture research: Seren Boyd, Amy Pimperton, Vernon Kingsley and Diana Morris

Picture credits: Africa Studio/Shutterstock: 28tl. Anneka/Shutterstock: 16-17 bg. Arcady/Shutterstock: 4tl bg. p bambaert/Shutterstock: 10tl. Julien Addington-Barker/Dreamstime: 12br. Lester V Bergman/Corbis via Getty Images: 20bl. Blan-k/Shutterstock: 15t, 20cr. Creative Icon Styles/Shutterstock: 12bc. dip/Shutterstock: 4b. Stephen Finn/Shutterstock: 18c. Foto-media/Shutterstock: 26-27 bg. Ishan Gercelman/Alamy: 29t. Pascal Guyot/AFP/Getty Images: 12bl. Richard Hanson: 11. Avinash Harpude/ephotocorp/Alamy: 24b. Ralph Hodgson: 5b, 7t, 9c, 10bl, 14bl, 16b, 17tr, 17b, 20tl, 21c, 22bl. imagegallery2/Alamy: 8b. InnervisionArt/Shutterstock: 12-13 bg. Irink/ShutterstockL 8tl. Itlada/Shutterstock: 22-23 bg. Marcel Janovic/Shutterstock: 8cr. Pavel K/Shutterstock: 27t. Vernon Kingsley: 25, 26. Thomas Koch/Shutterstock: 6cr. Georgios Kollidas/Shutterstock: 26tl. konstantiks/Shutterstock: 10tr. Kues/Shutterstock: 6-7 bg. Kuklos/Shutterstock: 14tl. Andrey Kuzmin/Shutterstock: 28 bg. Lakeview Images/Shutterstock: 24tl. LanKS/Shutterstock: 10-11 bg. laolaopui/Shutterstock: 15b. LovArt/Shutterstock: 24cr, 26c. lynx v/Shutterstock: 18cr. Malinka 1/Shutterstock: 17tl. Mauromod/Shutterstock: 4tr. Nejron Photo/Shutterstock: 18-19 bg. Olga Nikitina/Shutterstock: 14br. nikolae/Shutterstock: 14cr, 16c. Nine_Tomorrows/Shutterstock: 24-25 bg. Pakhnyushchy/Shuttesrtock: 14-15 bg. Atikan Pornchaiprasit/Shutterstock: 19b. Leigh Prather/Shutterstock: 20-21 bg. Tom Price: 19.

Jose Angel Aster Rocha/Shutterstock: 8-9 bg. Piyapong Rotnaparai/Dreamstime: 11bl. Walther S/Shutterstock: 5t, 10cr. Thaspoi Sangsee/Shutterstock: 6tl. Serg001/Shutterstock: 8cl, 10cl. Shaynepplstockphoto/Shutterstock: 4tl. Shtiel/Shutterstock: 16tl. Khrystyna Siasna/Shutterstock: 5c. singh lens/Shutterstock: 6b. sunchick/Shutterstock: 4-5 bg. Taipan Kid/Shutterstock: 12tl. M Taira/Shutterstock: 18tl. toadberry/Shutterstock: 29 bg. Toilet Twinning partners: 13t, 23bl, 27c. Top Vector Studio/Shutterstock: 24cl. Tribalium/Shutterstock: 6cl, 22c. Jim Vallee/Shutterstock: 21tc. vectorchef/Shutterstock: 7b, 9t,10br, 13b, 18b, 21tr, 22br, 27br. C Wisista/Shutterstock: 18cl. Natalia Yakovenko/Shutterstock: 4cl.

Every attempt has been made to clear copyright. For any inadvertent omission, please apply to the publisher for rectification.

ISBN: 978 1 5263 0375 2

Printed in China

Wayland
An imprint of
Hachette Children's Group
Part of Hodder and Stoughton
Carmelite House
50 Victoria Embankment
London EC4Y 0DZ

MIX
Paper from responsible sources
FSC® C104740
www.fsc.org